**NEWS FROM NOWHERE**
presents

# AN ○AK TREE

## by **tim crouch**

| | |
|---|---|
| **Co-directors** | **Tim Crouch, Karl James & a smith** |
| **Sound Designer** | **Peter Gill** |
| **Stage Manager** | **Mertan Mellon** |
| **Administrativ** | |
| Bach | |

Previewed at the Nationaltheater Mannheim, 29 April 2005
Premiered at the Traverse Theatre, Edinburgh, 5 August 2005

news from nowhere
www.newsfromnowhere.net

# CREDITS

## NEWS FROM NOWHERE

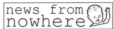

**News From Nowhere** was established in 2003 to help produce Tim Crouch's work. Its ambition is to explore the borders between theatre, visual art and education – through performance, teaching and commissioning.

To contact the company, e-mail: simon.martin@newsfromnowhere.net For more information, go to www.newsfromnowhere.net

## MADE IN BRIGHTON

**Made In Brighton** was formed in 2003 with the aim of discovering, supporting and investing in live theatre and creative talent by commissioning, guiding and championing ideas, individuals and producing companies. Its mission, in brief, is to transform Brighton from a receiving town, into a producing city.

www.madeinbrightonltd.com

 ⊙ Harbourfront centre

Supported by the Peggy Ramsay Foundation

# THANKS

Chris Dorley-Brown for his invaluable input at the early stages. The Peggy Ramsay Foundation for their support for the writing. Julia Collins. John Retallack. Jo Cole. Stuart at Ye White Hart, Barnes (a room above a pub). Thomas Kraus and staff at the Werkhaus, Nationaltheater Mannheim. Andrea Polanski. The David Knight Hypnotic Experience. Mark Ravenhill and Paines Plough. Michael Craig-Martin. Alister, Miranda and Dan at the Nightingale Theatre, Brighton. Alistair Creamer and all in Project Catalyst at Unilever. Annabel Turpin at Norden Farm Centre for the Arts. Jenny Harris and NT Education. Julia, Nel, Owen and Joe.

And to the second actors so far: Ian Golding, Cath Dyson, Hannah Ringham, Alex Miller, Tom Hartmann, Deborah Asante, Emma Kilbey, Dan Fordini, Alister O'loughlin, Jo Dagless, Matthew Scott, Anna Howitt, Natalie Childs…and all the ones to come.

# BIOGRAPHIES

## Tim Crouch (Writer/Co-director/Performer)

As an actor: co-founder and member of Public Parts Theatre (1986–1992); currently Associate Artist for Franklin Theatre, New York; extensive performance work in London and the UK, including *Endgame* in Brixton Prison, *Light Shining in Buckinghamshire* and *The Good Woman of Setzuan* for the National Theatre, where he is an Education Associate.

As a writer, Tim's first play, *My Arm*, opened at the Traverse during the Edinburgh Festival, 2003, and has subsequently toured nationally and internationally, with runs in New York and London. Since 2003, Tim has written and performed a trilogy of solo Shakespeare pieces for the Brighton Festival (*I Caliban*, *I Peaseblossom* and *I Banquo*) as well as a story-telling piece for the National Theatre, *Shopping for Shoes*, which has toured to schools throughout London. *An Oak Tree* is Tim's second play for adult audiences. Tim is currently Writer in Residence at the Nationaltheater Mannheim, Germany.

## Karl James (Co-director)

Karl was co-director and co-producer on Tim Crouch's first play *My Arm*. His early professional life was spent as an actor, composer and director working in the West End, at the Bristol Old Vic, Oxford Stage Company, Renaissance Theatre Company and Tiata Fahodzi. In 1996 Karl co-founded Trade Secrets, now one of the UK's most established arts-based training and development companies. In 2001, he started to focus his energies on a life-long passion and created The Dialogue Project, a company whose work is based on the belief that the world would be a better place if people were able to have healthier, more open-minded and productive conversations. As a result, he now spends most of his time working with people from different walks of life, in primary schools, boardrooms and rehearsal studios listening, thinking and talking.

www.thedialogueproject.com

## Peter Gill (Sound Designer)

Peter Gill is a classically trained composer, having studied violin at the Canberra School of Music, and later jazz at the renowned Canberra Jazz School. He is a founder member of the Deutsche-based production house PiXiEFiSH, with many releases to his credit within the record industry (including Ibiza classic, *Grooves and Vibes*). His work with the theatre began only recently in 2003 with the production *MONSTER* for Glasgow based company Visible Fictions. Peter currently lives in Brighton.

www.pixiefish.de

**Merritt Horton** (Stage Manager)

A graduate in dance from Stephens College in Columbia, Missouri, USA, Merritt went on to work in Boston for the Ballet Theatre and the Emerson Majestic. She has also worked at the Colston Hall, Bristol and for the Pleasance Theatre both in Edinburgh and in London. Merritt has worked at the Cochrane Theatre, London, and was resident technician at the Canal Café. She was technical manager of Newsrevue, and stage manager of *Mindbender* by Peeplykus, deputy stage manager for the Unicorn Theatre for Children's production of *Rama and Sita: Path of Flames*, company manager for *Hannah and Hanna* by Company of Angels and toured recently to Bologna, Italy with Theatre d'Lange Fou's production of *The Orpheus Complex*.

**a smith** (Co-director)

a smith is an artist who attempts to make accessible and poetic work. Most often employing forms of performance, writing and installation, this practice uses ideas of the everyday and social as its base, and builds itself from there. His recent projects have included *har du et minutt?/ do you have a minute?*, a piece commissioned for the Porsgrunn International Theatre festival, Norway, *The King and I* (with Catherine Dyson, BAC, London), and *The Disappearing Acts* (The Art Farm, Devon). Last year he completed the tenth and final part of *you are be a en*, a set of works about urban space and the city of London.

**Lisa Wolfe** (Administrative Producer)

Formerly Head of Marketing at Brighton Festival and Brighton Dome, Lisa has been a freelance arts project manager since 2001. Clients include Chichester Festival Theatre, South East Dance, Company of Angels, Polka Theatre, Komedia and Arts Council England.

# A NOTE FROM a smith

## Introduction

Hello. In your hand you are holding a play called *An Oak Tree*. It's by Tim Crouch. You are about to see it, or read it. Perhaps you have just watched it, or perhaps you saw it some time ago. Whichever it is, thanks for coming, or for showing an interest in the book and picking it up and taking a look. Welcome.

You can often find a bit of writing like this published with the text of a play. Sometimes it is referred to as the programme note. Its intention is to perhaps provide you the reader or audience member with some pearl of wisdom: supply a key that unlocks just a little of what you are about to see/read/have just seen/have just read/might just read/might buy/might put back on the bookshelf of the shop/other (delete where applicable). It might be that the note gives you the reader or audience member an outline of the story. Or maybe it gives some background information about the rehearsal processes, or the themes and form of the piece. It might even make reference to a significant incident in the life of the writer that has moved them to write it, or write in general. It may give you some ideas about what they wanted to say with this particular play. You may have realised by now that this may not be one of those programme notes. Of course, having not finished it, I don't know either.

## Information

I'm really glad I got the job of writing it, though. When I go and see plays and performances I always love reading these things. The anticipation! I sit there, waiting for the play to begin, attempting to absorb quickly all the stuff that I have mentioned. And sometimes afterwards I re-read the programme, and think about it in relation to what I have seen. It's so great to get an opportunity to write one!

You will have noticed, though, that I am having a bit of trouble with it. My problem is that I don't want to be presumptuous or complicated, and I don't want to reveal too much. I'm also getting distracted thinking about the other interesting information that is in this book too. Perhaps on the page before or after this there's a list of characters, or some biographies of the people who worked on the play. There's probably a list of thanks, those pages are so great to read too! If there's only a minute to go before the play begins, please don't think it would offend me if you want to look at those first. If you do, I'll just say thanks for reading this bit to here, and I hope you enjoy *An Oak Tree*.

Perhaps you've stuck with me (cheers!), or come back to carry on reading this afterwards (welcome back! What was the performance like tonight? Good, I hope). Perhaps you are reading the play now, some years after it happened. I am thinking about you too, standing there in a bookshop or library reading this introduction, trying to get an idea about what it's about and maybe even thinking about buying (or borrowing) it. Go on! You might have a great time, if reading plays is your thing.

## No lines

I am aware that you may be very dissatisfied with this programme note. 'It's not really telling me anything,' you might be thinking (or even remarking to your neighbour). I think it's a great privilege to be able to go and see plays and read about them in the programme note, but I just don't want to get into writing any of that problematic stuff about what the work means, does, or why it exists. I think that you are probably able to work that out by yourselves. So I am going to take this opportunity to tell you a story I have just remembered.

During a conversation about An Oak Tree in Germany[1], Tim Crouch said something about what he might have been thinking about when he was writing it. He said (and I am very aware that I may be paraphrasing him) that he wanted to think about a critical situation where he, or a character, might feel like they are performing in a play without a text, in scenes where they did not know the lines. At the time this seemed like an important thing, and it feels that for the purposes of this programme note it could be interesting to share it with you. I certainly think that it relates to the story that you are about to read/see (has the performance still not begun? what are they doing?). It also, I think, relates very strongly to the way the story is told.

You see, when we make and watch and talk about theatre we can have all sorts of conversations about the phenomena of it: about the live qualities of theatre, how it happens right in front of you, how we can move through space and time in different ways. We can talk about the reality of the theatre, about the truth of it, and how as well as being very real and here and now there might not be anything real at all here. For example, in this particular play you'll find a line I really like which talks about how you have all gone home, but you're actually still there! It's fascinating. Oh no! I said I didn't want to get into the problematic stuff!

But seeing as we have, before I go, what I would like to say is this: what I really hope is that plenty of these thoughts and conversations (and more) can be found in this play called *An Oak Tree*, and also that we can and should have them. Even more, though, I just want to say that I hope that you enjoy seeing or reading it. Thanks.

**a smith**

[1] I don't know if it is important that you know we were in Germany, but it certainly sounds impressive. Also, I love footnotes. They always seem to lend an importance to a piece of writing, even when they don't particularly say anything!

# EXCERPTS FROM...

## *an oak tree*
## 1973
## objects, water, and text
## collection: National Gallery of Australia
## by Michael Craig-Martin

*(There is a glass of water on a shelf. This is* An Oak Tree, *a work made by British artist Michael Craig-Martin in 1973. Beside the glass of water there is a text:)*

### Excerpt 1

Q. To begin with, could you describe this work?

A. Yes, of course. What I've done is change a glass of water into a full-grown oak tree without altering the accidents of the glass of water.

Q. The accidents?

A. Yes. The colour, feel, weight, size...

Q. Do you mean that the glass of water is a symbol of an oak tree?

A. No. It's not a symbol. I've changed the physical substance of the glass of water into that of an oak tree.

Q. It looks like a glass of water.

A. Of course it does. I didn't change its appearance. But it's not a glass of water, it's an oak tree.

### Excerpt 2

Q. Do you consider that changing the glass of water into an oak tree constitutes an art work?

A. Yes.

Q. What precisely is the art work? The glass of water?

A. There is no glass of water anymore.

Q. The process of change?

A. There is no process involved in the change.

Q. The oak tree?

A. Yes. The oak tree.

# AN OAK TREE

First published in 2005 by Oberon Books Ltd
521 Caledonian Road, London N7 9RH
Tel: 020 7607 3637 / Fax: 020 7607 3629
e-mail: oberon.books@btconnect.com
www.oberonbooks.com

Reprinted 2006

A catalogue record for this book is available from the British Library.

ISBN: 1 84002 603 0

Cover design by Julia Collins

Printed in Great Britain by Antony Rowe Ltd, Chippenham

*to Pam and Colin*

*'The distinction between fact and fiction is a late acquisition of rational thought – unknown to the unconscious, and largely ignored by the emotions.'*

*Arthur Koestler*

# Characters

HYPNOTIST

FATHER

# Notes

- *Eight chairs, stacked at the sides of the stage.*
  *One piano stool in the middle of the stage.*
  *Two handheld wireless microphones.*
  *An onstage sound-system and speakers.*

- *The actor playing the FATHER (the second actor) can be either male or female and of any adult age. They are completely unrehearsed in their role and walk on stage at the beginning with no knowledge of the play they are about to be in.*

- *This second actor wears Walkman/iPod headphones connected to a wireless receiver – this enables the HYPNOTIST to speak to and instruct the second actor through a microphone without the audience hearing. This script contains examples of these instructions but they are only given as guidelines: the actor playing the HYPNOTIST must pay detailed attention to these instructions to ensure a constant feeling of support and success for the second actor.*

- *Sections of script are prepared on clipboards. At times, the second actor, and sometimes the HYPNOTIST, read from these scripts.*

- *The Bach referred to in this script is the Aria from the Goldberg Variations. It is a flawed rendition: faltering but ambitious, failing to resolve until the very end of the play when it moves into the First Variation.*

- *Bold print indicates speech through a microphone.*

# Scene 1

*The HYPNOTIST brings the second actor on to the stage, introduces them to the audience, explains how they've never seen nor read the play, and then hands them a page of script. The second actor reads the part of the FATHER from the script.*

HYPNOTIST: Hello.

FATHER: Hello.

HYPNOTIST: Thanks for this.

FATHER: It's a pleasure.

HYPNOTIST: You hope!

FATHER: Yes!

*Pause.*

HYPNOTIST: How are you feeling?

FATHER: Okay.

HYPNOTIST: Nervous?

FATHER: A little.

HYPNOTIST: It'll be fine. You'll be fine.

FATHER: I'm sure.

HYPNOTIST: Any questions before we start?

FATHER: Not really.

HYPNOTIST: Nothing?

FATHER: How long is the show?

HYPNOTIST: The play?

FATHER: *An Oak Tree.*

HYPNOTIST: It's just over an hour.

FATHER: Okay.

HYPNOTIST: Anything else?

FATHER: Not really.

HYPNOTIST: Just say if you feel awkward or confused and we'll stop.

FATHER: Okay.

HYPNOTIST: Good.

Really good.

*The HYPNOTIST takes the FATHER's script from him / her.*

Look at me.

Look.

Ask me what I'm being, say: 'What are you being?'

FATHER: What are you being?

HYPNOTIST: I'm being a hypnotist.

Look.

I'm forty-one years old. I've got a red face, a bald head and bony shoulders. (*This must be an accurate description of the actor playing the HYPNOTIST.*)

Look.

I'm wearing these clothes.

Ask who you are, say: 'And me?'

FATHER: And me?

HYPNOTIST: You're a father. Your name's Andy.
You're forty-six, say, you're six foot two, say. Your
lips are cracked. Your fingernails are dirty. You're
wearing a crumpled Gore-Tex jacket. Your trousers
are muddy, say, your shoes are muddy. You have
tremors. You're unshaven. Your hair is greying. You
have a bloodshot eye.

That's great! You're doing really well!

Also, you'll volunteer for my hypnotism act. You'll
volunteer because I accidentally killed your eldest
daughter with my car and you think I may have
some answers to some questions you've been asking.
I won't recognise you because, in the three months
since the accident, you've changed. We've both
changed.

*Pause.*

There.

It doesn't get much harder than that, I promise.

Let's face out front. Ask who they are, say: 'And
them?'

FATHER: And them?

HYPNOTIST: They're upstairs in a pub near the
Oxford Road. It's this time next year, say.

Let's say they're all a bit pissed.

But don't worry, they're on your side. It's me they're after.

Face me.

I'll talk to them.

(*To the audience.*) In a short time I'll ask for volunteers but I'm not asking you. I'm asking some people in a pub a year from now. So don't get up.

(*To the FATHER.*) That's them dealt with!

Okay? Say: 'Yes.'

FATHER: Yes.

HYPNOTIST: Good.

Let's start. Take it easy. We're in no hurry.

Sit down there for the moment.

*The HYPNOTIST motions the FATHER to a chair in the audience.*

Good luck. I'm sure you'll be great.

Three. Two. One.

# Scene 2

*The HYPNOTIST puts on music.* Carmina Burana, *'O Fortuna'. Very loud.*

*During the music, the HYPNOTIST puts chairs into a row across the stage, with the piano stool in the middle.*

*The HYPNOTIST takes up his microphone.*

*'O Fortuna' ends.*

HYPNOTIST: **Ladies and gentlemen.**

**I will welcoming.**

**I will.**

**I.**

**Welcome you to this –**

**To my hypnotic world.**

**To my hypnotic world.**

**In a short minute's time I will be looking for such certain volunteers to come and join me here on this chairs these. These volunteers that they're –**

**Now, when before I ask these some hypnotic volun- superstars to come with join me, there is one are one or two things that I'd like to tell you about hypnotic about hypnosis, about stage hypnosis, about the things you're going to see tonight, or rather not rather not rather the things you'll never see in any of my shows.**

**Firstly. I will never lie to you. You will see no false nothing false tonight. Nothing phoney. No**

plants, no actors. The people you will see on stage tonight, ladies and gentlemen, apart from me, will be genuine volunteers.

You will be stars of the stars of this evening's –

Of all my shows all my shows are completely clean, ladies and gentlemen. Nobody will reveal any secrets tonight. In the shy, tonight, nothing nothing nobody will reveal any sexual fantasies tonight. There's no stripping in tonight's show. And there's absolutely no sex in at all in.

Sounds shit, doesn't it.

There is one are two types of peerson who cannot be volunteered hypnotised. The first type is anyone who is mentally unstable. If you're mentally unstable please do not volunteer for the for tonight's show. Also, in if you have asthma or the or ep-

epilepsy, please remain in your chair. Also, if there are any ladies here, ladies here who, ladies who are pregnant. If you are pregnant, congratulations, but please don't voluntise teer for tonight's show. There may be some ladies who are not pregnant but would like to be. Then come and see me after the show and I'll sort you out.

Now, in a few moments –

I've got about ten chairs. You will not reveal any secrets and you will not take your clothes off, but apart from that anything could happen.

Come up ladies and gentlemen and give me a piece of your mind.

I'm going to step back and play some music, and while the music's playing, if you have an open mind, if you're a game, you're game for a a laugh and you're over eighteen, then I'd like you to join me on this these chairs.

I'm going to stepping back.

I'm stepping back to let you come forward.

I'm going to play some music.

I'm just the hypnotist; you're the stars of the show.

Come up and give me a piece of your mind.

Your mind.

Your mind.

*The HYPNOTIST switches on cheesy 'come-on-down' music.*

*Music plays.*

*No volunteers.*

*The HYPNOTIST feeds instructions to the FATHER's headphones which bring the FATHER on to the stage and on to the piano stool.*

*Music stops.*

*The sound of passing road traffic.*

You're by the side of a road now, not far from here.

It's six thirty in the morning. You've been here for three hours. You're near a street lamp and you're next to a tree.

You're on the phone. Your mobile phone. You say, 'Marcy, Marcia, not now, baby.'

You say, 'Tell mummy it's me, darling, would you? Would you baby?'

*A lorry thunders past.*

You say, 'Dawn, love, I'm sorry. I'm sorry. I couldn't sleep. Dawn.'

You say, 'I'm weaker. I'm weaker than you.'

You say, 'She's here, love. She's here. I'm with her now.'

It starts to rain. Your face flushes with colour.

You say, 'Dawn. Dawn.'

You say, 'Fuck you.'

*The HYPNOTIST offers up his microphone to the FATHER.*

Say: 'Fuck you' into the microphone.

FATHER: **Fuck you**.

*A lorry thunders past.*

HYPNOTIST: The phone's dead. You're cold in this rain. By this tree.

Dawn will come to get you. She'll bring Marcy. She'll tell you that it's fucking freezing. She'll say it's a tree, Andy, it's just a fucking tree.

*Roadside sound stops as the HYPNOTIST switches on the cheesy music again.*

*The HYPNOTIST turns to an empty chair.*

HYPNOTIST: **Have you ever been hypnotised before, young lady?**

Sit on this chair and then say: 'No.'

*The HYPNOTIST offers his own microphone to pick up the FATHER's replies.*

FATHER: **No.**

HYPNOTIST: **Well there's a first time for everything. What's your name, gorgeous?** Say: 'Amanda.'

FATHER: **Amanda.**

HYPNOTIST: **Beautiful name for a beautiful girl. Isn't she beautiful, ladies and gentlemen? Sit back, Amanda, relax. That's it. You sir, what's your name?**

Move to this chair, say: 'Peter.'

FATHER: **Peter.**

HYPNOTIST: **You're a good-looking lad, isn't he, girls? A bit of eye candy for the ladies! Just relax, Peter. Great.**

**And you sir, what's your name?**

Move to this one, say: 'Lee.'

FATHER: Lee.

HYPNOTIST: **Peters and Lee!**

**You ever been hypnotised, Lee?**

Say: 'Yeah.'

FATHER: **Yeah.**

HYPNOTIST: **Hey, well you'll know when what you to do, won't you.**

Sit on this chair.

**What's your name, darling?**

Say: 'Jacqui,'

FATHER: **Jacqui.**

HYPNOTIST: **A bit nervous, Jacqui? Or maybe just a bit pissed!**

**Nothing to be nervous about. Just sit back, relax and enjoy!**

Move to the piano stool.

*The FATHER sits on the piano stool.*

**Although, Jacqui, it's HIM I'd be nervous of!**

**What's your name, mate?**

Say: 'Can I have a word?'

FATHER: **Can I have a word?**

HYPNOTIST: **Yeah, you can have a word, mate. 'Bollocks!' That's a word, isn't it. Got a right one there, ladies and gentlemen, haven't we? Going to have to keep our eyes on that one, aren't we?**

Sit here and smile out.

**I thought I said no one with a mental illness!**

**What's your name, mate?**

Say: 'Neil.'

FATHER: **Neil.**

*The HYPNOTIST kneels down.*

HYPNOTIST: **What's your name mate?!**

Say: 'Neil', again.

FATHER: **Neil.**

HYPNOTIST: **Your wife in, Neil?** Say: 'Wanker.'

FATHER: **Wanker.**

HYPNOTIST: **Right mate. Okay.**

Go and sit in the middle chair.

**Thank you, Neil, if you'd like to go back and join your party.**

*The HYPNOTIST puts 'Neil's' chair over on its side.*

**Ladies and gentlemen, Neil!**

**I'll let you in on a secret. I – I want this show to be a good one. I was doing a a a gig just last week. Everything brilliant. Everyone hypnotised. Everyone doing everything I suggested.**

**And just before the end of the show, I, er, I slipped off the stage, arse over tit. And the last thing I said before I landed was, 'Fuck me.' Couldn't sit down for a month.** A week.

*The HYPNOTIST stops the music.*

*The sound of the roadside is there.*

*The HYPNOTIST talks to the FATHER through headphones – inaudible to the audience.*

*'Slowly, over a count of ten, I want you to bring your arms out in front of you, as if you're hugging a tree.*

*'Fantastic. Just keep that position.*

*'When you hear music, I want you to slowly, slowly lower your right arm until it's hanging down by your side. And at the same time I want you to slowly, slowly, raise your left arm as high as you can. You can take about thirty seconds, a long time. Start moving your arms when the music begins. Your left arm will go up, your right arm will go down.'*

*The roadside sound stops as the HYPNOTIST switches on different music – hypnotic trance music.*

Now, I'm as as that weight is lowering your right hand I want to imagine that on your right hand I'm attaching, I mean your left hand, your right hand has a weight and on your left hand I'm attaching a helium-filled balloon. There, I'm tying a helium-filled balloon around your right left left wrist and I want you to imagine that your left arm is getting lighter and lighter and starting to float up. That's great, Shirley! Really good. Lighter and lighter. Fifty times lighter. Fifty times lighter.

No weight, Ian? Nothing? Not even – Thank you, if you'd like to go and rejoin the audience.

*The HYPNOTIST puts down an empty chair.*

Ladies and gentlemen, Ian!

*The FATHER's arms are getting more extreme.*

Eyes closed and just imagine. One arm getting heavier, the other starting to rise. Lighter and lighter.

That's it, just let yourself give yourself go to the to the image of the image that I'm giving you.

And really feel the weight of the weight and the lightness of the lightness. Fifty times heavier. Fifty times heavier –

All right. Great. No balloon, Jacqui?

It's fine. Only a bit of fun. If you'd like to rejoin your party. Ladies and gentlemen, Jacqui!

*The HYPNOTIST puts down another chair.*

Lee, was it? Nothing? If it's not there it's not there. Go back to the audience and rejoin your people. Ladies and gentlemen, Lee!

*The HYPNOTIST puts down another chair.*

All right, and stop. Stop it. Let's all just stop this, shall we? Open your eyes.

*The FATHER's arms are fixed in position. The HYPNOTIST gives the following instructions to the FATHER through his earpiece:*

*'Excellent. Hold that position. The Hypnotist will ask you to put your arm down, but I want you to just hold that position. Hold it until I say so. It won't be too long.'*

I said stop it.

*The HYPNOTIST stops the hypnotic trance music.*

Stop it. Put your arm down. Put your arm down. Now. He's funny, isn't he ladies and gentlemen? A bit of a joker.

You think you're very funny, don't you? A night out with your mates, get pissed up, have a laugh. Fuck around. We think it's funny, don't we? Don't we, ladies and gentlemen?

**What's your name, mate?**

Say: 'I can't move my arms.'

*The HYPNOTIST picks up the FATHER's replies with his microphone.*

FATHER: **I can't move my arms.**

HYPNOTIST: **Do you think I was born yesterday? Cut it out.**

Say: 'Can you untie me?'

FATHER: **Can you untie me?**

HYPNOTIST: **A right one here!**

**You having a laugh at me? Put your arm down, mate.**

Say: 'I can't move.'

FATHER: **I can't move.**

HYPNOTIST: **Stop fucking around. This bit's finished. Isn't it, Shirley? Peter?**

Look me in the eyes and say: 'Please help me.'

FATHER: **Please help me.**

*The sound of the roadside.*

*The HYPNOTIST gives the following instructions to the FATHER:*

*'Brilliant. You can relax your arms. You're doing really well. Take your time. Enjoy yourself. I want you to count to ten in your head, and then stand up.*

*'Now, in your own time lie down on the floor – on your back. Take your time.'*

*A lorry thunders past.*

*As the HYPNOTIST instructs the FATHER, he puts down three more chairs, until there are just three remaining – including the piano stool.*

*'Brilliant. Now we're going to have some fun! For the moment now, I want you to do exactly what the Hypnotist says. Just follow the Hypnotist's instructions.'*

*Hypnotic trance music starts again.*

HYPNOTIST: **...on a golden, sandy beach.**

**Beautiful. Lovely. Nice and relaxed.**

**And now, now, I want you to get up off the floor and go back to your chair on the stage. That's it. All three of you. And now, these chairs aren't your normal chairs, oh no. These are chairs at the Albert Hall. You're on stage at the Albert Hall. And I'm going to play some different music, and when the music starts all the ladies and gentlemen in the audience want to see you play the piano. Don't we, ladies and gentlemen? You're going to play the piano for the ladies and gentlemen. Nod your head if you understand.**

*The FATHER nods his head.*

*The HYPNOTIST stops the music.*

*Piano music plays. The HYPNOTIST gives the following instruction to the FATHER:*

*'Keep on playing. Play the piano and really get into it, enjoy it. Close your eyes if you like. When the Hypnotist says "sleep" that's when you stop. The Hypnotist saying "sleep" is your cue to stop. When you stop, just drop your head down.'*

*The HYPNOTIST puts down the remaining two chairs.*

*'Aren't you going to play for the ladies and gentlemen, Shirley? No piano, Peter, nothing? If you'd like to return to the audience. etc.'*

*Only the FATHER playing the piano on the piano stool is left. The moment is held.*

**What's he doing, ladies and gentlemen? What is he doing? Someone put you up to this? Is this a trick, a joke, is it?**

**You're not convincing. You're not believable. We can see you're trying it on, can't we, ladies and gentlemen? We just want to forget about it, don't we, turn back to our drinks. Don't you, ladies and gentlemen? They know this isn't a piano, you know this isn't a piano. There's no piano there. There was never a piano. You can't do this. We don't believe you. You can't – You can't. Stop it. STOP IT.**

**And sleep.**

*The HYPNOTIST stops the piano music.*

**Bit of a wanker, here, ladies and gentleman. Thinks he's a bit of a star. Friend of yours, is he? Anyone know him? Nobody? Shall we have a bit of fun, eh? See what he's really made of, stop him fucking about. Shall we? Because we all know he's only putting it on, don't we? We all know somebody's put him up to this.**

**Open your eyes, mate.**

**Listen, mate. I'm going to count down from three. And when I get to one, you'll look down and you'll**

see that you're bollock naked. Absolutely starkers, in front of all the ladies and gentlemen. Nod your head if you understand.

Nod your head.

And not only that, but when you hear this sound (*A fart sound.*) you'll be convinced that you've shit yourself. That warm shit is running down the back of your naked leg. Nod your head if you understand.

And then – And then, when I click my fingers, you'll become convinced you've done something terrible, and you'll feel really guilty – truly terrible, ladies and gentlemen. When I click my fingers, you'll be convinced convinced that you've killed someone. You've killed a little girl, a girl, haven't you, and you'll feel really awful. A little girl. Nod your head if you understand.

This should be fun, shouldn't it, ladies and gentlemen? We're looking forward to it, aren't we?

And, three, two...

*The HYPNOTIST gives instructions directly to the FATHER through the earphones:*

*'The Hypnotist is really going to humiliate himself now, and say some pretty horrible things to you. Play along with it; but you don't need to act it out. I'll do all the work. Your cue to stop is "sleep". On "sleep", stop what you're doing.'*

...one.

*Music plays. A ghastly, jaunty, clownish music.*

Hey, mate, stand up. Oh, where are all your clothes? Eh? Ladies present, mate. Show a bit of respect. And, oh, look at your little chap. Cold out, is it? Where is he, won't he come out to play? That must be a bit embarrassing. (*Makes a farting noise.*) Oh, dear, mate, what's happened there, eh? Oh dear, that's a bad smell. Couldn't you have waited? Urgh, all down your leg and all. How do you feel about that? Pretty bad, eh? Pretty apologetic towards me, I imagine. And to everyone. Stinking up the place with your stinky shit. Like you want to say sorry, I should think.

Say: 'Sorry.'

FATHER: **Sorry.**

HYPNOTIST: **Louder.**

FATHER: **Sorry.**

HYPNOTIST: **Say: 'Sorry for my stinky shit.'**

FATHER: **Sorry for my stinky shit.**

*The HYPNOTIST clicks his fingers.*

HYPNOTIST: **And what about that kid. A girl, was it? Didn't see her coming? Driving along, were you? Drive along. Put your hands on the wheel. Drive. Look at you, you're driving! Turn and wave at the audience as you drive your car along.**

*The HYPNOTIST gets the FATHER to mime driving.*

She wasn't looking, was she? Here she is, a little girl, here she is. And there's you in your car. Just stepped out, didn't she? Look out, mate, look where you're going! Look out for that girl. Look out! Oh, and she's dead! You killed her! Think of her little body. Think of her poor mummy and daddy. Just driving along, were you? How does that make you feel? What do you wish you were? I bet you wish you were dead! Say it. What do you wish? You wish you were dead. Say: 'I wish I was dead.' SAY IT.

FATHER: **I wish I was dead.**

HYPNOTIST: **Louder.**

FATHER: **I wish I was dead.**

HYPNOTIST: **What?**

FATHER: **I wish I was dead.**

HYPNOTIST: Keep driving along, keep waving to the audience and keep telling the audience that you wish you were dead until I say 'sleep'. Keep going, even when the music stops.

FATHER: I wish I was dead, I wish I was dead... (*Etc.*)

HYPNOTIST: **All right. Enough. Stop. STOP. FUCKING STOP THIS.**

*The HYPNOTIST stops the clownish music. The FATHER keeps driving an imaginary car and keeps saying 'I wish I was dead.' The moment is held.*

**And SLEEP.**

**What are you doing? What's happening? Why are you doing this? What are you doing here? Why are you here?**

Say: 'I'm Andrew Smith.'

FATHER: **I'm Andrew Smith.**

33

HYPNOTIST: Say: 'I'm Claire's dad.'

FATHER: **I'm Claire's dad.**

HYPNOTIST: Say: 'The girl.'

FATHER: **The girl.**

*The Bach plays and stops.*

HYPNOTIST: Oh Jesus. Oh God.

*An audible instruction is given immediately:*

*'I'm going to fall to my knees now. The music will play. Just watch me.'*

*The HYPNOTIST falls to his knees.*

*Bach plays and stops.*

*Bach plays. During it, the HYPNOTIST sets up and instructs the FATHER for the next scene.*

*The HYPNOTIST gives the following instruction:*

*'Great. I'm going to get us some script.*

*'We're going to read together when this piano music ends. You'll read the part of the Father. Let's stand here. Just face out and read. Take your time.'*

*Bach stops.*

# Scene 3

*The HYPNOTIST and the FATHER stand side by side. Both read from scripts.*

HYPNOTIST: That evening. Dusk.

FATHER: That evening.

Watching Claire leave – her Walkman on, sheet music stuffed into a bag. A five minute walk to the lesson.

Dusk.

HYPNOTIST: This was my route. A fiftieth birthday party in a sports hall. I had to phone and cancel. I said there'd been an accident, but I didn't give details.

FATHER: That night. That night has a colour, a touch and a sound. Dawn was back. We waited supper for Claire. Marcy was watching *The Simpsons.*

Blue. We waited supper in blue. We brushed against each other in slate grey. We looked at our watches in yellow.

HYPNOTIST: I was driving a Renault Laguna estate. 1.6 litres. The car was good. The brakes were good. ABS. Airbags. In the back, speakers, sound-board, microphones, costumes. My lights were on. November.

FATHER: Our pulses raced in purple. We phoned the piano teacher in brown. Our stomachs knotted in green. The policeman walked up the path in red. We watched him from the window in orange. He took off his hat at the door in gold.

White. Dawn's knees gave way in white.

HYPNOTIST: This is the point on the map. This is the Ordnance Survey grid reference. This is the bend on the road. These are the leaves by the kerb.

FATHER: Death. Death walked through into the lounge. He put his helmet on the piano stool, spoke to us in silver. He then pronounced two concrete blocks in black and left them to hang inside my ribcage, pushing against my lungs. Where they remain to this day. Recently I asked Dawn if she thought I should go to the doctors to arrange to have them removed. 'Where's my man?' she screamed. 'Where's my fucking husband gone?'

HYPNOTIST: These are the yellow lines, the white lines. This is the quality of the light. This is the tree by the verge. This is the view from the North. This is the view from the South. This is my hand, reaching down for a cigarette. For a second. At thirty-seven, thirty-eight, thirty-nine. In the dusk. This is the girl. Her Walkman on. Some piano music. On the way to her lesson.

*Bach plays and stops.*

*Bach plays. The HYPNOTIST feeds the following instructions to the FATHER:*

*'I'm going to get a bit more script. Stay there.*

*'We're going back to the end of the previous scene, with me on my knees. So stand where you were and we're going to start this scene when the piano ends. Take your time, enjoy it. You're doing really well.'*

# Scene 4

*The HYPNOTIST goes down on his knees.*

*The Bach stops.*

*The FATHER reads from his script.*

HYPNOTIST: Look, let's get out of here. I'll buy you a drink. I had no idea you were –

FATHER: A drink of what? What?

HYPNOTIST: Look. This isn't the best –

We should find somewhere more – Hang on. Let me talk to the audience.

**Ladies and gentlemen.**

**I'd like to apologise for – If you'd be kind to wait just a few moments, I'm happy to refund your tickets. In the meantime, I can only apologise – Please, this performance is now over. The bar is open.**

Look, let me give you my – we can – I need to –

FATHER: I'm sorry.

HYPNOTIST: No, no. It's me. I'm – As you can see, things haven't been going too well. I'm just honouring old bookings. It's not –

FATHER: I need to wipe this up –

HYPNOTIST: What?

Indicate the back of your legs and say: 'This.'

FATHER: This.

HYPNOTIST: I don't understand.

FATHER: I'm so sorry. I don't know what happened.
I need a towel or something, something to cover
– In front of all these people. I don't know what
happened. It's not like me.

HYPNOTIST: What?

Indicate the backs of your legs again and say: 'This.'

FATHER: This.

HYPNOTIST: No. There's nothing. It was a suggestion.
There's nothing there. You didn't –

You're fully clothed.

There's no mess. It was me. I was doing it. I
hypnotised you. I put you under.

I didn't think you'd – I thought nobody had – I
thought you were taking the piss. People take the
piss. I didn't recognise you. It's been three months
since –

FATHER: No. Look. I'm dirty. I need –

HYPNOTIST: No. I'm sorry.

FATHER: Yes. Smell. I feel awful. This is not –

HYPNOTIST: Yes. Yes. All right. I'm sorry. You're
naked. You have shit down your legs.

FATHER: Yes. I'm sorry.

HYPNOTIST: Listen. Listen.

Here. Let me clean you up. Here, with this cloth.

This is the right kind of cloth, isn't it? Say: 'Yes.'

FATHER: Yes.

HYPNOTIST: Soon get you clean.

Stand here and face straight out.

*The HYPNOTIST wipes the back of the FATHER's legs with an imaginary cloth.*

There.

FATHER: I'm sorry about the girl.

HYPNOTIST: What?

FATHER: The girl I killed. What was her name?

HYPNOTIST: What?

FATHER: The girl I killed. You said.

HYPNOTIST: No. No, that was – That was me. You didn't –

There was no girl.

FATHER: Yes.

HYPNOTIST: Yes, there was, but not you. You did nothing. Me. It was me. You did nothing.

I killed someone. You know that. That's why you're here. Why you volunteered.

FATHER: I'm sorry. I wanted to enjoy the show. I didn't mean to spoil it for you.

HYPNOTIST: Please. You didn't. Really. Since November, I –

FATHER: November?

HYPNOTIST: Since your daughter's death, I've not
– I'm not. I've not been much of a hypnotist.

FATHER: I saw your poster. I recognised your name.
When I saw what you did, I was interested. I thought
you could help. Will you help? I need help.

My wife – Dawn – she's very unhappy.

I'm so sorry about this.

HYPNOTIST: It's fine. These things happen. It's not
your fault. Here.

*The HYPNOTIST takes away the FATHER's script.*

Now you're clean. Look, see. Clean. The smell has
gone. Has the smell gone?

Say: 'Yes.'

FATHER: Yes.

HYPNOTIST: Good. That's really good.

Face me.

Now I'm going to put some clothes on you. They're
probably not your choice of – I mean, these are just
things I've – But let's get you covered up.

*The HYPNOTIST starts to clothe the FATHER with
imaginary clothes.*

Legs in. That's it. Well done. These are good trousers,
aren't they? Say: 'Yes.'

FATHER: Yes.

HYPNOTIST: There was no girl you killed. No girl. Do
you understand? No girl.

It was a game. I was being stupid. I was angry.

Arms out. That's it. This is a nice shirt, isn't it? It's green, isn't it? Yes? Say: 'Yes.'

FATHER: Yes.

HYPNOTIST: And this pattern, it's good, isn't it? Say: 'Yes.'

FATHER: Yes.

HYPNOTIST: Good. All dressed now. All better now? Yes? Say: 'Yes.'

FATHER: Yes.

*The HYPNOTIST hands the script back to the FATHER.*

HYPNOTIST: From here.

You're all clean and put back together.

FATHER: Yes, I'm all put back together.

HYPNOTIST: Let's get you home.

FATHER: No.

HYPNOTIST: But –

FATHER: I wanted to see you. I wanted to talk to you at the – since the funeral. But I didn't know how to find you. I wanted to say something.

HYPNOTIST: Andrew.

FATHER: Andy.

HYPNOTIST: Andy,

There's really nothing I – At the inquest – It wasn't my fault. Your daughter was listening to music. She didn't – I –

FATHER: No, it's not like that. I'm not here because – I wanted to – I needed you to know.

Claire's fine.

HYPNOTIST: What do you mean?

FATHER: She's fine. I mean she's okay.

She's not okay.

I mean I found her –

I haven't found her.

Only.

You have to help me.

I've done something.

Something impossible.

And I don't know how I did it.

Something miraculous.

But it's not good.

It's no good.

And I don't know what to do.

I don't know what to do.

Will you help me?

*Bach plays.*

*The HYPNOTIST gives the following instructions directly to the FATHER:*

*'Now I'm going to feed some lines to you through your headphones. Just stand here, face out, and deliver the lines to the audience. We'll start when this piano music ends. You're doing brilliantly.'*

*Bach stops.*

# Scene 5

*The following speech is prompted throughout by the HYPNOTIST who speaks inaudibly into a microphone, but whose words are picked up through the FATHER's headphones.*

FATHER: Ladies and gentlemen.

Dawn went to the mortuary. I refused. If anything, in those first few days, Claire had multiplied. She had become cloned! She was between lines, inside circles, hiding beneath angles. She was indentations in time, physical depressions, imperfections on surfaces, the spaces beneath chairs, surrounding blunt pencils, inside plastic buckets.

Ladies and gentlemen.

Dawn was diminished. She clung to material evidence. To her, Claire was a hair left on a bar of soap, some flowers taped to a lamp-post. She was the photograph framed and hung above the piano. For me, these things were no more of Claire than of anyone else. A photograph just looked like other photographs. Whilst I had the real thing!

Nod your head if you understand.

The house began to fill with grief. After the inquest, the undertakers appeared. Dawn and Marcy discussed which of Claire's cuddlies should go into the coffin. On the day of the funeral I went for a walk. Dawn screamed at me, but I had no one to bury.

Nod your head if you understand.

I came to the roadside. I needed a hug from my girl.
I looked at a tree. A tree by the road. I touched it.
And from the spaces, the hollows, the depressions,
I scooped up the properties of Claire and changed
the physical substance of the tree into that of my
daughter.

Three. Two. One.

*Bach plays.*

*The HYPNOTIST instructs the FATHER through the
headphones:*

*'Once the music has stopped, I'll ask you if you're okay.
I'll say, 'Are you okay?' When I ask you this question,
take your earphones out and let them hang down, and
ask me for a drink of water. Say: 'Could I have a drink
of water, please?'*

*Bach stops.*

# Scene 6

HYPNOTIST: Are you okay?

*The FATHER takes out his earphones.*

FATHER: Could I have a drink of water, please?

HYPNOTIST: Yes, yes. Of course. I'm so sorry. Here.
Here. I'll go down to the bar and get you one. I'll be
no longer than thirty seconds, I promise. Will you be
okay on your own? Say: 'Yes.'

FATHER: Yes.

*The HYPNOTIST exits the stage to get a glass of water
for the FATHER. He is gone no more than thirty seconds,
leaving the FATHER alone on stage with the audience.
The sound of the roadside. Sound stops.*

*The HYPNOTIST returns with a glass of water and
hands it to the FATHER.*

HYPNOTIST: Would you sit on the piano stool?

*The HYPNOTIST hands the FATHER a new piece of
script.*

You're doing brilliantly.

How are you feeling about it?

FATHER: Fine.

HYPNOTIST: Not embarrassed?

FATHER: A bit.

HYPNOTIST: You should have said, I'd have stopped.

FATHER: It's okay.

HYPNOTIST: Still nervous?

FATHER: A bit.

HYPNOTIST: It doesn't show.

I thought I saw you struggling to keep a straight face earlier on.

FATHER: Yes.

HYPNOTIST: When was that?

Was it around the wiping up the shit? People usually get the giggles around then.

FATHER: No, actually.

HYPNOTIST: When?

FATHER: When you said Renault Laguna. I used to drive a Renault Laguna.

HYPNOTIST: How funny!

What do you think's going to happen?

FATHER: I don't know.

HYPNOTIST: Who's your favourite character?

FATHER: Nobody really.

HYPNOTIST: Do you get the story?

FATHER: About the girl?

HYPNOTIST: I suppose so.

FATHER: I get that she's dead. Or is that all in his mind?

HYPNOTIST: Whose?

FATHER: Mine. The father's.

HYPNOTIST: No, she really is dead.

FATHER: And you killed her?

HYPNOTIST: Indirectly, yes.

FATHER: I don't understand the stuff with the tree, then.

HYPNOTIST: No.

FATHER: I feel sorry for his wife.

HYPNOTIST: Dawn?

FATHER: And his other daughter. The one who's watching *The Simpsons*.

HYPNOTIST: Marcia.

FATHER: How old is she meant to be?

HYPNOTIST: I don't know. Whatever you think.

FATHER: I think she's about five?

HYPNOTIST: Five's good. She's a bit under-written.

FATHER: Yes.

Do we ever get to see her?

HYPNOTIST: She appears as a chair.

FATHER: Okay.

Could I ask a question about my character?

HYPNOTIST: Of course.

FATHER: What does he do for a living?

HYPNOTIST: I've always assumed he's a teacher.

FATHER: Okay.

Of art or something?

HYPNOTIST: I always assumed Maths, or Geography.

FATHER: Oh.

HYPNOTIST: Is it important?

FATHER: No.

HYPNOTIST: Are you okay if we get back to it?

FATHER: Of course.

HYPNOTIST: You're really good. You're doing really well.

FATHER: So are you. It's really well written.

HYPNOTIST: Thanks.

Go and sit back in the audience.

FATHER: In the pub?

HYPNOTIST: Yes.

FATHER: But they've all gone.

HYPNOTIST: Yes. The show was a failure; they became embarrassed and left. It's what I'm used to. Don't worry on my behalf. For the last three months, since the accident, I've been – I've lost all ability. Like I said, honouring old bookings.

FATHER: I'm sorry.

HYPNOTIST: I've lost my mojo! Have to think about a career change. Could be worse, I could be dead!

Sorry. I'm so sorry.

FATHER: It's fine. It's not really me.

HYPNOTIST: Of course not.

FATHER: And anyway, it hasn't happened yet.

HYPNOTIST: What?

FATHER: You said it's a year from now.

HYPNOTIST: Yes! Of course.

FATHER: You will help me, though, won't you?

HYPNOTIST: I don't see what I can –

FATHER: Dawn says I need closure.

HYPNOTIST: I'm not really a therapist.

FATHER: I've thought about suicide.

HYPNOTIST: I –

Okay?

*The HYPNOTIST motions the FATHER to sit down in the audience again.*

Thank you.

Three. Two. One.

# Scene 7

*Music plays loud. The 'come-on-down' music from the HYPNOTIST's act.*

*During the music, the HYPNOTIST instructs the FATHER to come up on stage and to sit on the piano stool. He provides the FATHER with a script and a microphone and instructs him/her directly on what to do.*

*The HYPNOTIST picks up another chair and places it behind the FATHER's piano stool, where the HYPNOTIST will sit, his back to the FATHER and the audience.*

*Music stops.*

FATHER: Dawn.

Dawn.

HYPNOTIST: Sssh.

FATHER: Dawn.

HYPNOTIST: What?

FATHER: You still crying?

HYPNOTIST: I'd just got to sleep. I was sleeping.

FATHER: I wanted to read something to you.

HYPNOTIST: You'll wake Marcy.

FATHER: Help you to relax. It's from one of the books
  – the books they left – You don't have to do anything.

HYPNOTIST: I can't stand this. I was asleep, Andy.

FATHER: Listen. It's a script. It will help you.

HYPNOTIST: Please.

*The FATHER will read the following speech through a microphone. At the same time, the HYPNOTIST will get increasingly distraught and upset, delivering Dawn's words over the FATHER's speech.*

*Gradually the 'hypnotic' music from the stage act starts to be heard – playing from the same place as the Bach and the roadside. This will build slowly throughout.*

FATHER: **'I want you to imagine that you are lying on a golden sandy beach. And as you lie under the warmth of the sun, I want you to feel all the muscles in your body are beginning to relax. All the tension is beginning to melt away.'**

HYPNOTIST: I can't bear this.

FATHER: **'Your heels are sinking gently into the soft, warm sand.'**

HYPNOTIST: Stop this, Andy, please. What's happening?

FATHER: **'Your ankles, your calves, the backs of your knees, your thighs, your buttocks, your sacrum, the small of your back, your spine sinks down, vertebrae by vertebrae, your ribcage, your shoulders, the nape of the neck, the back of the neck, your head.'**

HYPNOTIST: Has it not sunk in yet? Is that what's happened? Well it had better soon, because I can't do this on my own. I can't stand this. It's three o'clock in the morning, Andy, and our beautiful daughter is lying in a fridge somewhere and you're asking me to relax my fucking knees.

FATHER: **'Sinking further and further, relaxing deeper and deeper. All tension bleeding out of your body and into the golden sands. As you breathe in and out, in and out, I want you to be receptive to the thought that you're letting go of all anxiety, fear, sadness, anger, grief or any other feeling and emotion that is holding you back.'**

HYPNOTIST: Don't you go mad on me, man. I need you. This is hell. If it wasn't for Marcy I'd be under a car. I'd be at the bottom of a lake, off a bridge, under a train, hanging from a fucking beam. Don't you feel it? Oh God, oh God. You don't get it. Claire's gone, Andy. She's gone.

FATHER: **'You're breathing now in rhythm with the waves that are gently lapping at your feet. The water is clear and sparkling. It is glinting in the dappled sunshine. As the water plays around your body you begin to make a conscious connection from your heart to the whole of creation. And as you breathe, you feel your body sinking lower and lower into the sand, at all times supported by the earth that is so rich, so abundant, so unconditional that her energies can provide you with all you're asking for.'**

HYPNOTIST: You're not even listening. It's like some abstract intellectual fucking concept for you, isn't it? Claire's death. She never existed for you in the first place. She was just some idea. The idea of a daughter, just as I'm the idea of a wife. Marcy's the idea of a child. We don't exist for you, do we, not in flesh and blood. So you haven't lost anything, have you? She's still there, in your head, where she was in the first fucking place. Well I have. I fucking have. Help me.

FATHER: **'Here begin to create the intention of collecting the subtle qualities you require to help you on your life's journeys, such as balance, health, clarity, courage. Be aware that as the waters lap around you, your body sinks under and is redeemed of all loss, all negativity. And when at last the waters recede, they leave you feeling completely refreshed and totally relaxed.**

*The trance music stops.*

**'These are instructions for a mental exercise. Practise each day for one hour. Use caution in releasing yourself at the end of each period of exercise.'**

*Bach plays. The HYPNOTIST instructs the FATHER.*

*Bach stops.*

You've woken Marcy.

HYPNOTIST: I need to clear this up. Pack the car.

*The HYPNOTIST starts to put the chairs back into the configuration they were in at the beginning – stacked on either side, with the piano stool still in the middle.*

All this stuff is mine, the speakers – I suppose I should sell it. I sold that Laguna.

FATHER: Do I stay here? Do I stay sitting?

HYPNOTIST: I don't know.

FATHER: You said I was doing brilliantly.

HYPNOTIST: You are.

FATHER: You said we could stop if I wasn't enjoying it.

HYPNOTIST: That was just a thing to say, to encourage you.

FATHER: I want to stop.

HYPNOTIST: Listen.

She just stepped out. That's all. I went round to the front of the car. You could still hear the music from her Walkman.

FATHER: She could really play.

HYPNOTIST: I'm sure she could.

FATHER: I loved to listen to her, watch her fingers.

HYPNOTIST: I have to go, Andy. Or they'll kick us out.

FATHER: And then tonight!

I couldn't play before tonight. Didn't know I could play.

I was good, wasn't I?

HYPNOTIST: Stand up.

Stand here.

*The HYPNOTIST positions the FATHER in relation to the piano stool and takes away his script.*

You're cold in this rain.

Three, two, one.

*The sound of the roadside.*

*The HYPNOTIST is there, holding a chair on his hip, as he would a five year-old girl.*

Are you coming home?

Come home, it's fucking freezing.

You say, 'I can't leave.'

I say, 'She's not here.' You say, 'You can't see.'

I say, 'Where then? Where is she?' You say, 'Here. Here.'

I say, 'It's a tree, Andy. It's just a fucking tree.' You say, 'No, you're wrong.'

I say, 'It's all right, Marcy. Daddy's poorly. Oh, you're frozen, you poor thing. Let's get you home.'

I say, 'Look, she's lost her sister. She's not going to lose her fucking father, too.'

I say, 'We all have to deal with this. Cope with this. We have to get on. See things for what they are.'

Point at the piano stool.

Say: 'Look, Dawn, look.'

FATHER: Look, Dawn, look.

HYPNOTIST: Say: 'It's not a tree anymore.'

FATHER: It's not a tree anymore.

HYPNOTIST: Say: 'You're not looking.'

FATHER: You're not looking.

HYPNOTIST: Say: 'I've changed it into Claire.'

FATHER: I've changed it into Claire.

HYPNOTIST: I say, 'Our girl is dead, love. She's dead.'

I say, 'That is a tree, I am your wife, this is your daughter, that is a road. This is what matters. This. This is what we have to deal with. This.'

*The sound of a lorry thundering past.*

*The roadside noise ends.*

*The HYPNOTIST gets the FATHER to sit on the chair that was playing Marcia and hands him a script. The HYPNOTIST then sits in the seat in the audience.*

Is it how you imagined it?

FATHER: What?

HYPNOTIST: Doing this.

FATHER: The whole coming on stage thing?

HYPNOTIST: Yes, the whole thing.

FATHER: I didn't really know what to expect.

HYPNOTIST: Why did you agree?

FATHER: It sounded interesting.

HYPNOTIST: Don't you think it's a bit contrived?

FATHER: Hard to tell from here.

HYPNOTIST: Of course.

Have you seen any of my other work?

FATHER: No.

Also –

Dawn says it's as though there's been two deaths.
She says if I don't sort my head out soon she's taking
Marcy.

So I ought to do something.

I think it's because I never went to the morgue.

If I'd been able to see her for one last time. If I'd said
goodbye.

And when I saw your name on a poster.

HYPNOTIST: You thought I could help?

FATHER: Say: 'I have to pack up.'

HYPNOTIST: I have to pack up.

*The HYPNOTIST switches off the onstage sound
equipment. He sits on the piano stool, next to the
FATHER.*

You know there wasn't a piano.

FATHER: What?

HYPNOTIST: Earlier. There wasn't really a piano.

FATHER: Yes. I played it. I played it earlier on.

HYPNOTIST: No. That was just me playing some
music and saying that there was.

FATHER: No. I really played it.

# Scene 8

*Music plays, loud.* Carmina Burana, *'O Fortuna'.*

*As the music plays, the HYPNOTIST gives a series of instructions to the FATHER.*

*'O Fortuna' cuts out. Both actors read from scripts. As the two actors read, the Bach begins to play.*

HYPNOTIST: When I say so, you're driving.

It's dusk. The sky is purple, blue, orange, yellow, grey.

To your right, the rim of the world is blackening.

You're on your way to somewhere. You're not too tired.

You shift your weight. You shift your weight again.

You glance at the mirror. You catch sight of the upper left-hand corner of your face.

You're forty-one.

You're driving forward in space and time.

FATHER: When I say so, you're walking.

It's dusk.

You're on your way to somewhere. You shift your weight. You shift your weight again.

You're twelve.

The air is cold. You're listening to music. You're not too tired.

You're walking forward in space and time.

HYPNOTIST: When I count to three, you're cornering. You're reaching for a cigarette.

Nod your head if you understand.

FATHER: When I count to three you're dreaming of winter and supper and *Futurama.* Your cheeks are flushed with the cold.

Nod your head if you understand.

HYPNOTIST: When I click my fingers, you're swerving. Your hands are gripping the steering wheel, your foot is jabbing hard on the brakes.

FATHER: When I click my fingers, you're stepping off the kerb.

HYPNOTIST: When I say 'sleep', a girl is there. Her eyes are wide open.

When I say 'sleep', she looks at you.

When I say 'sleep', everything slows.

FATHER: When I say 'sleep', a car is coming towards you. You're listening to music.

When I say 'sleep', the music stops.

HYPNOTIST: When I say 'sleep', she lifts her hand up.

When I say 'sleep', you say goodbye.

FATHER: When I say 'sleep', everything stops.

HYPNOTIST: Sleep.

FATHER: Sleep.

HYPNOTIST: When you open your eyes.

FATHER: When you open your eyes.

*The music passes through into the First Variation, which plays through to an end.*

*Blackout.*

*End.*